DISGUSTING & DREADFUL SCIENCE

Gut-Wrenching Gravity

and other fatal forces

by Anna Claybourne

W

FRANKLIN WATTS

LONDON • SYDNEY

First published in 2013 by Franklin Watts

Copyright © Franklin Watts 2013

Franklin Watts
338 Euston Road
London NW1 3BH

Franklin Watts Australia
Level 17/207 Kent Street,
Sydney, NSW 2000

Produced by Penny Worms & Graham Rich, Book Packagers

A CIP catalogue record for this book is available from the British Library.

Dewey Decimal Classification Number: 531.1

ISBN 978 1 4451 1479 8

Printed in China

Franklin Watts is a division of Hachette Children's Books, an Hachette UK company.

www.hachette.co.uk

Picture credits
Corbis images: 17b (Justin Paget). **fotolia:** 4b (Eduard Härkönen), 16t (Dan Moller), 18b (Nickolae), 19t and cover (sarah5), 26b (pegbes), 26t (Henrik Larsson), 27tl (Dmitry Ersler), 27tr (Thomas Beitz). **Getty images:** 25b (AFP/ Fabrice Coffrini), 24t (The Image Bank/Windsor & Wiehahn). **iStockphoto.com:** title page (Dean Murray), eyeball cartoon (Elaine Barker), 4r (jesse christoffersen), 5b (pidjoe), 7bl (CactuSoup), 8l (Eric Isselée), 8r (hudiemm), 9t (Ugurhan Betin), 9br (TriggerPhoto), 10b (Sébastien Decoret), 10t and cover (Aleksander Trankov), 11b (Linda Bucklin), 13b and cover (Sven Hermann), 20t (Christian Martínez Kempin), 22t (Tommounsey), 23b (Nikada). **NASA:** 14b, 19bl, 27bl, 28t, 28b, 29b. **Science Photo Library:** 15r (Victor Habbick Visions), 29t (Mark Williamson). **Shutterstock.com:** angry monster cartoon (Yayayoyo), 5tr and cover (Philippe Ingels), 5tl (Africa Studio), 6–7 (HomeArt), 7tr (Sergej Khakimullin), 9 mouse (Don Purcell), 11t (Kapu), 12b and cover (jabiru), 14t (CoraMax), 15b (Yingko), 18t (Nickolay Vinokurov), 21c (Joe Belanger), 21t (grafoto), 21b (Stuart Elflett), 23c (xpixel), 24b (creativedoxfoto). **Wikimedia:** 11 – Louis XVI, 13r, 25t.
All other illustrations by Graham Rich

Every attempt has been made to clear copyright. Should there be any inadvertent omission, please apply to the publisher for rectification.

Contents

Feel the force!

Oops! CRUNCH! Ouch! If you trip over your shoelaces and go flying, you soon fall flat on your face. You are dragged violently towards the ground by a fearsome force called gravity. Gravity acts like a **PULLING** force. So when you fall over, you really are being pulled to the ground.

We'll force you!

Gravity is just one of the forces that pull, push, squeeze and shove us around, all day long. We're so used to them, we often don't notice them – but they affect everything we do.
Here are a few you might recognise...

PUSH – when you kick a ball, you push it with your foot

PULL – when you pull your socks up to get them onto your feet

SQUEEZE – when you SQUELCH a handful of slime between your fingers

STRE-E-ETCH – when you pull an elastic band, then ping it across the room

SCRAPE – when your chair scrapes on the floor with an ear-splitting screech!

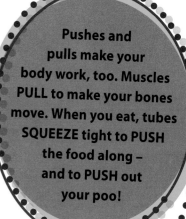

Pushes and pulls make your body work, too. Muscles PULL to make your bones move. When you eat, tubes SQUEEZE tight to PUSH the food along – and to PUSH out your poo!

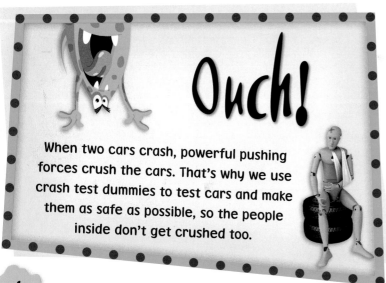

Ouch!

When two cars crash, powerful pushing forces crush the cars. That's why we use crash test dummies to test cars and make them as safe as possible, so the people inside don't get crushed too.

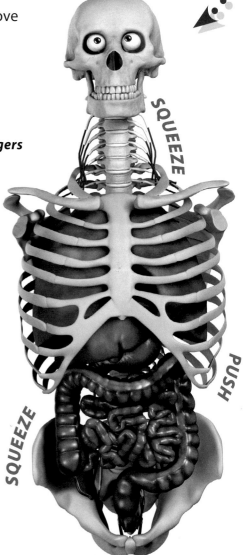

SQUEEZE

PUSH

SQUEEZE

Balanced forces

If an object isn't moving, it's because the forces acting on it are balanced. If a cake sits on a plate, gravity is pulling it down, but the plate is in the way and stops the cake from falling. The plate is actually pushing it up. The two forces balance each other and the cake stays still.

 ## See for Yourself

Diving board

Hold a wooden or plastic ruler on the edge of a table, and stand a toy figure on the end. Gently pull down the tip of the ruler, then let it go.

You PULL down on the ruler. The ruler springs back and PUSHES the figure up. After a daring leap, gravity PULLS the figure to the ground.

Wheee!

Unbalanced forces

Who do you think will win this arm wrestle?

If the pushing forces are unbalanced, the stronger force will push the weaker one.

The mystery of gravity

Gravity is everywhere. It makes an egg splat on the floor when you drop it. It makes snot dribble out of your nose. It lets you pour juice into a glass, play ball games and have a shower. Gravity can be a drag when you're carrying a heavy bag, but it can be fun too, when you're sledging, skiing or skydiving.

I'm floating away!

Imagine life without gravity! Nothing would stay where you put it. You couldn't walk down the street – you'd just float around. The air would be filled with random objects. Except there wouldn't be any air, either! Gravity holds air in place around our planet, allowing us to breathe. So, as you can see, it's pretty important.

6

A universe of gravity

Everything on Earth (right) is pulled towards the centre of the planet by gravity, but it's not just the Earth that has gravity. Every object – including the Moon, a pebble, a pea, and you yourself – has a pulling force that draws it towards other objects. The more massive an object is, the more powerful its gravity. Small objects have such weak gravity we don't notice it, but Earth's gravity is so strong it pulls on us and everything else nearby.

On Earth, there's actually no such thing as 'down'.

How does it do it?

How can one object pull on another across empty space? Where exactly does the pulling power of gravity come from? The truth is... wait for it... we don't actually know! Gravity is a massive mystery. The world's greatest minds are still trying to figure out why it's there and how it works.

Yuck!

Scientists have found that when toast falls off a table, it really does usually land on the buttery side. That's because, as it tips off the table, it starts to spin. In the time it takes gravity to pull the toast to the floor, it only has time to spin 180 degrees, or half a full turn – so it's upside-down when it lands.

Splatttt!

Splat!

Stand back! Cow dung (below) can make a mighty splat as it hits the ground! The further something falls, the bigger the mess when it lands. As an object falls towards the Earth, it speeds up, or accelerates. The longer it falls for, the faster it falls. That's why you can jump off a low wall and land safely (most of the time!) but what if you fell off a high cliff?

Yuck!

Some birds use the splatting power of gravity to help them bombard their enemies with sticky, slimy droppings.

Faster... faster... faster

On Earth, falling objects speed up by 9.8 metres per second, for every second that goes by. That's quite a lot – equivalent to about 35 km/h. With each second that passes, the object falls 35 km/h faster. As you can imagine, after just a few seconds, a falling object is zooming as fast as a speeding train.

Floaty and Fluffy

The speed of a falling object is affected by air resistance – that is, air getting in its way. Light, fluffy objects like feathers catch a lot of air, which slows them down, but a rock or a person falls much faster. If there was no air resistance, a feather and a rock would fall at the same speed.

Drop it!

Imagine you climbed up a 100-metre skyscraper, and dropped a rotten tomato off the top.
Look out below!

AFTER 1 SECOND
Your tomato is already moving faster than you could run! It's falling at
35 km/h

AFTER 2 SECONDS
It's just past
70 km/h

AFTER 3 SECONDS
It's plummeting down at almost
106 km/h

AFTER 4 SECONDS
Your tomato is travelling at a breakneck speed of
140 km/h
Then it hits the ground...
SPLAT!

DID YOU KNOW?

A mouse could fall off the same skyscraper and survive unharmed. Even though it would land at a scary speed of over 140 km/h, the mouse isn't heavy enough for this to damage its body.

See for Yourself

Water balloon splats

Fill several balloons with water (use the same amount of water for each one) and tie them closed. Then try dropping them from different heights off the ground – 0.5 metres, 1 metre and 1.5 metres (*you'll need to go outside for this!*)
How far does a balloon have to fall to make it splat?
Can you make a bigger splat by dropping it from higher up?
To get your balloons even higher, throw them up in the air.

Record your results on a chart, like this.

	Height	Diameter of splat
1st drop	0.5 m	No splat
2nd drop	1 m	?
3rd drop	1.5 m	?
4th drop	3 m	?

Don't forget to clean up the bits of balloon afterwards. They can be hazardous to wildlife.

9

Deadly gravity

Living with gravity can be **DREADFULLY** dangerous. Whether it's you falling over, or something falling on top of you, gravity's pulling force can cause all kinds of deadly disasters.

Aarrrrggghhhh!

Base jumpers and skydivers throw themselves out of aeroplanes or off cliffs and mountains for fun. Falls of more than about 15 metres without a parachute are usually deadly for humans, but some people are lucky. During the Second World War (1939-45), British Royal Air Force gunner Nick Alkemade jumped from his burning plane. He fell about 5,500 metres and prepared to die. Instead, a pine tree broke his fall and he landed in soft snow. He was unhurt except for a sprained ankle.

A skydiver in free fall, enjoying the pull of Earth's gravity.

Falling from space

Sometimes, bits of rock flying through space come close enough to the Earth to be pulled in by its gravity. They often burn up as they fall through the atmosphere and we see them as 'shooting stars'. Some, called meteorites, fall all the way to Earth. If they hit someone, it could be deadly. In 2009, a pea-sized meteorite hit 14-year-old Gerrit Blank as he walked to school in Germany – luckily he wasn't badly hurt. If a really big space rock, or asteroid (left), hit us it could wipe out life on Earth!

10

DANGER AVALANCHE

Get out of the way!

Gravity often causes terrifying natural disasters. It pulls floodwater, avalanches, landslides and frazzling hot volcanic lava downhill. The further they flow, the faster they go, flattening anything in their path.

Snow might be fun, but an avalanche is terrifying and deadly when it's hurtling towards you at over 160 km/h!

Fatal fall

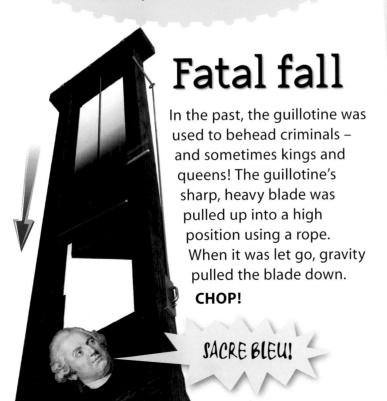

In the past, the guillotine was used to behead criminals – and sometimes kings and queens! The guillotine's sharp, heavy blade was pulled up into a high position using a rope. When it was let go, gravity pulled the blade down. **CHOP!**

SACRE BLEU!

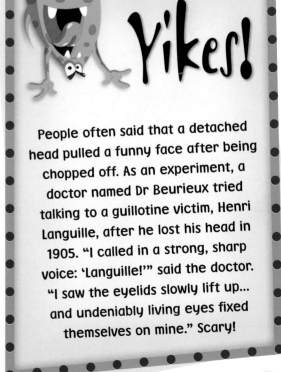

Yikes!

People often said that a detached head pulled a funny face after being chopped off. As an experiment, a doctor named Dr Beurieux tried talking to a guillotine victim, Henri Languille, after he lost his head in 1905. "I called in a strong, sharp voice: 'Languille!'" said the doctor. "I saw the eyelids slowly lift up... and undeniably living eyes fixed themselves on mine." Scary!

Gut-wrenching g-forces

You might have heard of fighter pilots and racing drivers enduring massive 'g-forces'. Strong g-forces can make you feel dizzy, throw up, collapse unconscious, and even die! So, what are they?

See for Yourself

Feel supergravity

Try jumping and landing again on bathroom scales *(Be careful! Just do a small jump so you don't break them)*. Look at the scales as you land and you'll see them showing an increased reading, as you decelerate and your g-force goes up. The same thing happens sometimes when you're in a lift and it lands on the ground floor.

Extra gravity

The 'g' in g-force stands for gravity and 1g means the force of gravity you feel on Earth. A force of 2g means twice the force of Earth's gravity, and so on. When you accelerate (speed up) or decelerate (slow down), you feel a pushing force. In an aeroplane, you feel 'pushed' back into your seat at take off. On a bus, you are pushed forward if it stops suddenly. These are g-forces. When we experience them, we feel a force greater than gravity.

Wheeee!

You experience g-forces when you swoop up and down on a rollercoaster, or when you're in a car that turns a corner, pushing you sideways. If you fall, then hit the ground, your body experiences multiple gs as you suddenly decelerate.

AAGGGHHH!

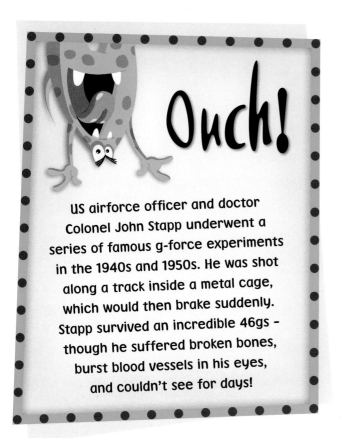

Ouch!

US airforce officer and doctor Colonel John Stapp underwent a series of famous g-force experiments in the 1940s and 1950s. He was shot along a track inside a metal cage, which would then brake suddenly. Stapp survived an incredible 46gs – though he suffered broken bones, burst blood vessels in his eyes, and couldn't see for days!

1

John Stapp bravely enduring super-high g-forces in the name of science.

2

3

SUPER-G STATS

Space shuttle during a launch	3g
Rollercoaster	3–5g
Formula-1 racing car turning	up to 6g
Fighter jet turning	up to 12g
Car crash at 50 km/h	25g

G-force machine!

Pilots of fast planes undergo high g-forces as they accelerate, twist and turn. To help them get used to it, they are whirled around in a human centrifuge machine, which spins faster than any fairground ride to create huge g-forces. As the gs increase, the pilot first suffers 'grey-out' (loss of colour vision), then tunnel vision, complete blindness, and finally 'GLOC' – g-force induced loss of consciousness. **Urgh!**

High g-forces are all in a day's work for fighter pilots and racing car drivers.

Falling forever

Imagine falling... and falling... and falling... but never hitting the ground! Well, that's what Planet Earth is doing right now and it's taking you with it. We are orbiting around the Sun and orbiting is basically falling. It happens because of gravity.

Moon's forward motion

Pull of Earth's gravity

Resulting path (orbit)

How does it work?

Think of our Moon orbiting around us. The Moon moves at a certain speed, but it is also close enough to the planet to be pulled by its gravity. The Moon is constantly trying to keep going in a straight line, but the planet's gravity pulls on it, making it fall in towards it. These two forces balance each other out, and the Moon ends up moving around and around the planet – always falling, but never landing.

The same forces are also at work on the International Space Station and astronauts, such as this one, on spacewalks.

Gravity glue

Gravity holds the whole solar system together. The huge Sun is in the middle, and its mighty gravity holds the planets in orbit. The planets each have their own moon or moons orbiting around them.

See for Yourself

Make a moon

You can see how a moon's orbit works by whirling a ball on a string. Tie a string about 50 cm long to a plastic ball. Use sticky tape to hold it in place if necessary. Whirl the ball around (first making sure no one is in the way). The speed of the ball makes it pull away from you. But the string acts like gravity, holding the ball in place. It ends up moving around in a circle.

The big squeeze

One of Jupiter's moons, Io (right), is like a big zit. Jupiter's super-strong gravity squeezes it so much it squirts out goop from inside through its many volcanoes.

Ouch!

Medieval weapons like the chain mace used orbiting forces, too. The chain held the mace ball, while it whirled around at great speed, before making contact with someone's head!

Stretched into spaghetti

Earth's gravity is strong. Jupiter's gravity is stronger. The Sun's gravity is stronger still. But to experience the most powerful gravity of all, you'd have to brave something much stranger – the mysterious depths of a black hole.

Black holes sound scary - what if the Earth gets sucked into one? Don't panic! The nearest black holes are many millions of kilometres away and, although their gravity is very strong, they only pull in objects that get close enough.

What's a black hole?

Black holes (above) are strange space objects where gravity is taken to the extreme. They suck in space dust, gas, comets, bits of stars, and even light. Their gravity is so strong that nothing that gets sucked in can ever escape. Instead, it all gets squashed together more and more tightly, until it's smaller than a pinprick – but heavier than a star. Mindboggling!

Where do black holes come from?

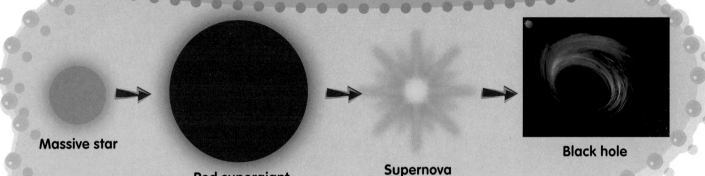

Massive star

Red supergiant

Supernova

Black hole

A black hole forms when a very big star runs out of fuel. At the end of its life it expands to form a red supergiant, then explodes (a supernova) as its gravity makes it collapse in on itself. It pulls itself into a clump of matter that is very dense – meaning it's very heavy for its size. Its strong gravity sucks in more and more matter, until it becomes a black hole. Black holes get their name because they even suck in light, so they appear as blackness.

Getting sucked in

Slurp! Slurp!

If you fell into a black hole feet first, the super-strong gravity would pull harder on your feet than on your head, as your feet would be nearest to it. This would make your body stretch as you got sucked in – an effect scientists call 'spaghettification'. Luckily, though, no one has actually fallen into a black hole... yet!

See for Yourself

The plugholes of space

Run some water into a sink, then take the plug out.

As the water swirls down the plughole, sprinkle some glitter and a few tiny bits of tissue paper around it.

You'll see them swirl around the hole and move faster and faster as they get sucked in. A black hole works in a similar way. Scientists can't see them, but they can detect them from the way nearby objects move around the black hole.

Gravity geeks

We may not yet understand gravity completely but we know a lot more than we used to. That's thanks to the brilliant brains of these gravity-studying geniuses.

Mind your head!

People used to think heavy objects fell faster than light objects. Some light objects, like feathers, do fall slowly, but this is because of air resistance – air getting trapped and holding them up. The great scientist Galileo saw that, if it wasn't for air resistance, gravity should pull all objects at the same rate. In 1589, according to legend, he tried dropping two weights, one ten times heavier than the other, off the Leaning Tower of Pisa (right). He proved his point! As they were both solid and heavy, air resistance had little effect, and they both landed at the same time.

Over to Isaac

Galileo died in 1642, and in that same year Isaac Newton was born. Newton was probably the most brilliant boffin ever. He worked out that gravity made orbits work, and that everything had gravity, not just the Earth. Some people say he 'discovered' gravity when an apple fell on his head – but of course everyone already knew that objects fell downwards. They just didn't understand what was going on in the same way Newton did.

Isaac Newton (1642–1727)

18

Ouch!

Bonk! The story of an apple landing on Newton's head is famous, but it may not be true. Newton himself said that seeing apples falling in his mother's garden made him think about gravity, but he didn't say they fell on his head. He simply questioned why they didn't fall sideways or upwards, but always towards the Earth's centre.

Einstein

The great physicist Albert Einstein said that gravity happens because matter bends space and time, so that smaller objects fall 'in' towards it. It's hard to understand, but this experiment might help...

Moon test

When the first astronauts walked on the Moon (above), they tested Galileo's theory. They dropped a metal weight and a feather to test whether they fell at the same speed when there was no air resistance at all. They both landed at the same time, just as Galileo predicted they would.

See for Yourself

Bending space

Try testing Einstein's idea by stretching out a piece of stretchy fabric over the top of a big bowl. Secure it tightly with a large elastic band or tape. Put a big marble in the centre of the fabric. What happens? Try rolling marbles of different sizes and weights across the fabric. Can you explain what is happening and why?

The big marble is like a planet bending space (the stretchy fabric). The smaller marbles (a moon or an asteroid or a spacecraft) 'fall in' when they get close enough to the planet's gravity.

Note: This experiment uses a flat surface, but in reality the 'bending' would work in all directions.

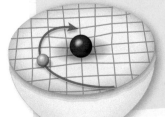

Frightening friction

Friction is a dragging force that happens when things rub against each other. It can cause some painful injuries, like when you scrape your knee, get a massive blister from your shoe, or burn your hands sliding down a rope – OUCH! But if it weren't for friction, every day would be like walking on ice!

But what is friction?

Friction happens when two surfaces are in contact and trying to move past each other. They catch and rub, and slow each other down. This can damage them, and it also uses up energy. Rough or squashy surfaces, like sandpaper and rubber, have more friction. Smooth, shiny surfaces, like glass, have less.

Yuck!

When things are covered with water, oil or slime, there's less friction because the liquid gets between the two surfaces. For example, snails make slippery slime to help them slither along the ground. Deep-sea hagfish release lots of slime to make it harder for predators to grab and catch them.

A snail's slime helps it to overcome friction, but wheels are even better!

Wheels make it easier to move around because they don't rub – they roll instead, making friction less of a problem.

Friction and heat

When friction happens, some of the movement energy gets turned into heat, and the surfaces warm up. That's why you rub your hands together to warm them on a cold day. Heat from friction is used to strike matches, and also lets you start a fire by rubbing sticks together.

Racing cars use smooth tyres in dry weather, and tyres with rough treads in the rain, to give them extra friction.

 ## See for Yourself

Feel the heat

1. Take two identical coins and put them both on a pad of paper. Hold one still, and rub the other one quickly to and fro for 30 seconds. Which one ends up warmer?

Without friction

2. Fill a large, smooth plastic fizzy drink bottle with water, dry it, and see if you can hold it up in one hand. Now spread a thin layer of vegetable oil all over it. Is it still as easy to hold?

Magnet mayhem

A magnet can defy gravity. It can pull objects up towards it, or push another magnet into the air. So the force of magnetism can actually make things seem to 'float' instead of falling. How does it do that?

What is a magnet?

A magnet is an object – usually a metal bar, disc or U-shape – that has a magnetic field – an area of force around it. It can attract, or pull, some things towards it – especially anything made of iron, steel or nickel. Two magnets can attract each other, or repel (push away from) each other. Just like gravity, these forces can reach across empty space.

Magnets sometimes occur naturally. They can also be made from a magnetic material such as iron. In a magnet, the atoms – the tiny parts that all things are made of – are arranged in a regular pattern that gives the magnet its force. A flow of electricity can also create a magnetic force.

A magnetic bar picking up thousands of tiny iron filings

Magnets

One end of a magnet is called the **north pole** and the other is called the **south pole.** When two magnets are put together, north and south ends will pull together and connect. If you try to put two south poles or two north poles together, they push away. They will not connect.

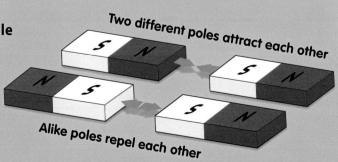

Two different poles attract each other

Alike poles repel each other

22

North pole? South pole? Do those terms sound familiar? That's because the Earth is a giant magnet too, and has its own North Pole and South Pole.

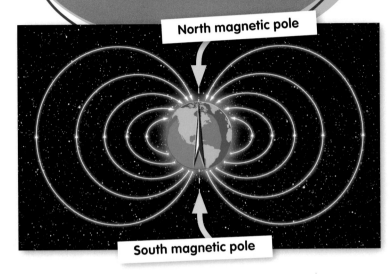

North magnetic pole

South magnetic pole

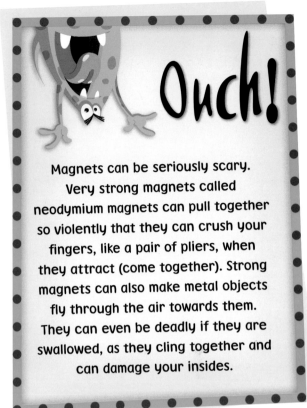

Ouch!

Magnets can be seriously scary. Very strong magnets called neodymium magnets can pull together so violently that they can crush your fingers, like a pair of pliers, when they attract (come together). Strong magnets can also make metal objects fly through the air towards them. They can even be deadly if they are swallowed, as they cling together and can damage your insides.

MRI

An MRI scanner uses magnetism to make chemicals in your body change position, then turns their movements into an image. It's often used to scan people's brains.

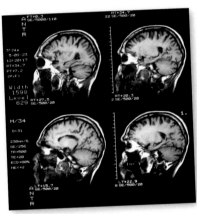

An MRI brain scan

Beware the power!

A super-speedy 'maglev' train (left) uses magnets to help it move. Strong magnetic forces make the train hover above a magnetic rail, so friction never slows it down. Other magnets, powered by electricity, make the train move. Similar technology could be used in the future to move other things around too. In the *X-Men* comics and films, the villain Magneto uses his magnetic powers as a weapon, and to control huge metal objects like ships – though this doesn't happen in real life (yet!).

Floating, flying and gravity-defying

 Humans have always longed to leave the ground, like birds and insects do. It took us a long time, but we eventually invented several ways to defy gravity and fly.

Personal jet-packs – the future or just a dream?

See for Yourself

Flying hands

Planes fly because the wings are slightly tilted. As they zoom forward, air hits the underside of the wing and is pushed down. This pushes the plane up.

To demonstrate this, use a hairdryer on a cool setting to blow air at your hand.

First, hold your hand out flat.

Now try tilting your hand like this. Can you feel it being pushed up by the airflow? This is how aircraft wings get pushed up too.

 COOL AIR!

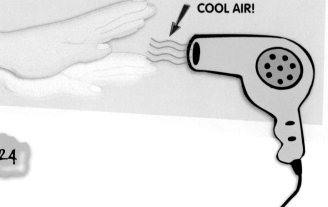

Hot air!

The first passenger-carrying flying machine, a huge hot-air balloon, took to the air in 1783. Hot-air balloons work by floating. Cold air is heavier than hot air, so cold air sinks down (pulled by gravity), and pushes hot air up. If the balloon is big enough, and the air inside is hot enough, it can carry people into the sky.

Balloons and airships are sometimes filled with lighter-than-air gases, such as helium. Like hot air, these gases make the balloon float upwards, while the heavier air sinks down.

Wonderful wings

Long ago, people tried to fly by copying birds and building big, flapping wings – but they were too heavy and didn't work. When inventors tried using fixed, spread-out wings, like a gliding eagle, aeroplanes were born. The first planes were gliders with no engines – they were launched off hills.

Otto Lilienthal was known as the Glider King for his fantastic flying machines.

Ouch!

In 1507, an inventor named John Damian made himself a pair of wings from eagle and chicken feathers. He tried to fly from the top of a tower but fell straight into a sloppy, stinky dungheap!

Is it a bird? Is it a plane?

This superhuman-looking high-speed flyer is actually pilot and inventor Yves Rossy, wearing his custom-built, jet-engine-powered wing suit. His invention lets one person fly like a bird, but only he has flown in it so far. It works like a miniature plane, with fixed wings that allow it to fly and glide. In 2008, Rossy used his flying suit to cross the English Channel, a journey of 35 km.

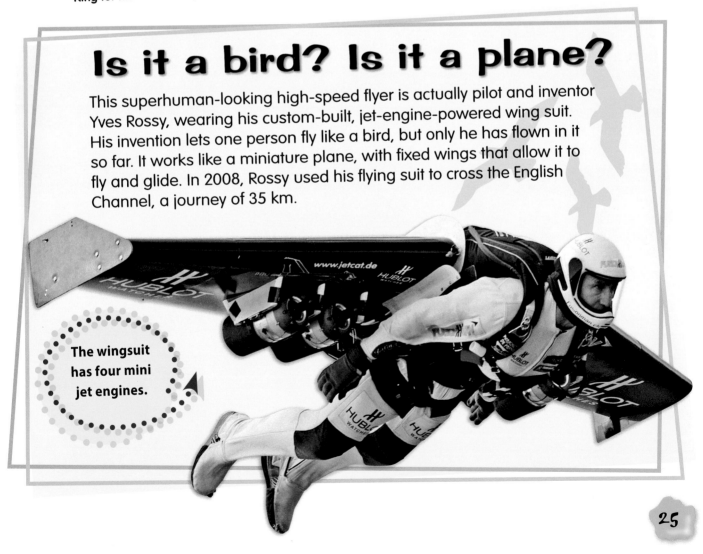

The wingsuit has four mini jet engines.

Crawling on the ceiling

If gravity affects everything on Earth, how do spiders, flies and lizards crawl across the ceiling? Have you ever wondered that? After all, we can't walk on walls and ceilings. So what have creepy-crawlies got that we haven't?

Even if a wall looks smooth, it will probably have tiny bumps and cracks in it. Spiders have tiny claws on their feet that they use to cling onto them. As a spider is very light, and has eight legs to use, it can usually get a good grip. But spiders walk up windows too.
How do they do that?

A spider can have over 70,000 tiny hairs on each foot.

Gripping hairs!

Through a microscope you'd see that spiders' feet are covered in tiny hairs. Each of these hairs has hundreds of tinier hairs, called setae. But how do hairs help?

When you touch a surface with your fingertip, you don't actually touch much of it at all. Your finger and the surface have different textures, and close-up, only some parts actually touch. When a spider touches a surface with its hairy feet, each tiny hair makes contact.

AAGGGHH!

Sticking power

Weak electrical forces, called Van der Waals forces, attract surfaces together. They are so weak we rarely feel them, but the hairs on a spider's feet make such close contact with a surface, the Van der Waals forces are strong enough to make it stick. Gecko's feet are hairy too, and work in the same way.

GECKO toes!

Besides being covered in tiny setae, a gecko's toes are wide and rounded, to give them a bigger gripping area.

Gecko's toe hairs (setae) —

Gecko's toe

Surface

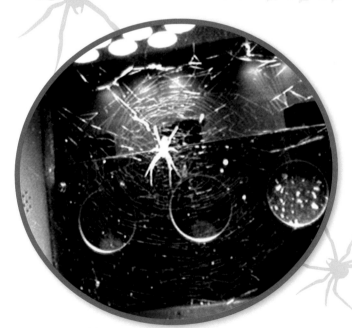

Spiders in space!

Spiders have been sent into space aboard rockets to see if they could still spin their webs in zero gravity (above). They could!

Yuck!

If you've ever walked into a cobweb, you'll know it's stretchy, sticky and icky! Spiders use their silk to spin webs and catch prey, but also to hang down from ceilings. To fix the silk to a ceiling, a spider wraps several threads into a sticky bundle called an attachment disk, and presses it into place. Then it dangles from the other end. Watch out!

All aboard the vomit comet!

Flying is amazing when you think about it – being thousands of metres in the air in a small metal tube with wings, eating and drinking and watching TV. But imagine what it would be like to experience ZERO gravity* and float around almost weightless.

*Ahem!

There's actually no such thing as true zero gravity. Gravity gets weaker and weaker with distance, but it never disappears completely. All objects have their own gravity, so we are never free of it. The correct term for very low gravity is 'microgravity'.

Yuck!

On the International Space Station, astronauts stay for so long, they can't take all their drinking water with them. Instead, they have a system that cleans and recycles their urine so they can drink it again!

Into space

Astronauts in orbit experience microgravity on their missions (top). Floating around and doing somersaults is fun, but space can also be seriously messy. Any spilt food or drink ends up flying around all over the place (above).

Astronaut poo!

So how do astronauts go to the toilet? Imagine everything from your toilet at home floating around all over the room! Space toilets solve this problem using a suction system. As you sit on the toilet, air is sucked out of it, and everything else gets sucked away too. The poo is dried out, then stored in a sealed container to be taken back to Earth.

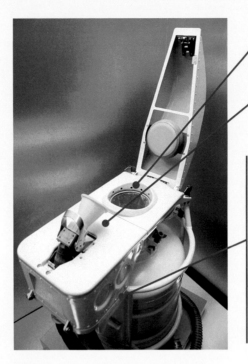

- This is the hole for 'solid' waste (that's poo).

- This is the urine funnel. It's flexible so men can wee standing up and women can wee sitting down. This 'liquid' waste is treated and recycled.

- Air suction does the job that gravity does on Earth. It pulls the waste into the toilet.
- A fan separates the waste from the air using centrifugal force.
- The air is treated to remove odours and bacteria before it is released back into the room.
- The solid waste goes into plastic bags inside the toilet, which are squashed flat.

The vomit comet

WWHHHEEEEEE!

The vomit comet is the nickname for a plane that can create a gravity-free experience for trainee astronauts. It works by climbing up high, then plummeting downwards at the same speed as free fall. The people inside are falling, but the plane is falling with them – so, for a few minutes, it is just like being weightless inside a spacecraft.

Why 'vomit comet'? Because the experience of weightlessness often makes people horribly sick. Everyone is given a special vomit bag, just in case!

BLEUURRGGH!

Glossary

accelerate to speed up

air resistance air that is in the way of a moving object slowing it down

asteroid a rocky space object that orbits the Sun

atoms tiny units that all things are made of

attract to pull on something

base jumpers people who jump off objects, such as mountains and buildings, wearing wingsuits and parachutes

behead to cut someone's head off

black hole a space object with very strong gravity that sucks nearby material into it

decelerate to slow down

force a push or pull acting on an object

g-force the force of gravity or acceleration on an object

guillotine a machine for beheading people using a falling blade

maglev (short for magnetic

levitation) a type of train that uses magnetic force to move and to hover above the track

matter the stuff that makes up objects and substances

meteorite a lump of rock or metal from space that falls and lands on the Earth's surface

microgravity very low gravity

orbit to circle around an object, held in place by its gravity

physicist a scientist who studies physics

physics the science of forces, energy and matter

repel to push something away

solar system the Sun and all the planets and other space objects that orbit around it

spaghettification a stretching effect that acts on objects that are sucked into a black hole

tunnel vision being able to see only a small area right in front of you

Van der Waals force a weak pulling force between objects

Websites and Places to visit

NASA Kids' Club
www.nasa.gov/audience/forkids/kidsclub/
flash/index.html
Lots of fun activities and facts about space exploration, rockets and astronauts

Microgravity water balloons
spaceflightsystems.grc.nasa.gov/
WaterBalloon
A series of cool videos showing how water behaves in microgravity

Science Kids – Forces in Action
www.sciencekids.co.nz/gamesactivities/
forcesinaction.html
An interactive truck game that lets you experiment with friction and other forces

Zoom Science – Forces & Energy
pbskids.org/zoom/activities/sci
The Forces & Energy section has lots of fun and fascinating force-related experiments to try.

thinktank
Birmingham Science Museum and Planetarium
Millennium Point, Curzon Street,
Birmingham B4 7XG
www.thinktank.ac

At-Bristol
Anchor Road, Harbourside,
Bristol BS1 5DB
www.at-bristol.org.uk

Science Museum
Exhibition Road, South Kensington,
London SW7 2DD, UK
www.sciencemuseum.org.uk

Glasgow Science Centre
50 Pacific Quay,
Glasgow G51 1EA, UK
www.gsc.org.uk

MOSI
Museum of Science and Industry
Liverpool Road, Castlefield,
Manchester M3 4FP
http://www.mosi.org.uk

Magna Science Adventure Centre
Sheffield Road, Templeborough,
Rotherham S60 1DX
www.visitmagna.co.uk

Spaceport
Victoria Place, Seacombe, Wallasey,
Wirral CH44 6QY
www.spaceport.org.uk

Smithsonian National Air and Space Museum
National Mall Building:
Independence Avenue at 6th Street,
SW Washington, DC 20560, USA

Steven F. Udvar-Hazy Center:
14390 Air and Space Museum Parkway, Chantilly, VA 20151, USA
www.nasm.si.edu

Index